P9-DBT-127

TYRABANKS

TYRABANKS

FROM SUPERMODEL TO ROLE MODEL

ANNE E. HILL

LERNER PUBLICATIONS COMPANY · MINNEAPOLIS

For George, Caleb, and Abby, my inspirations for everything.

The images in this book are used with the permission of: © iStockphoto.com/yhloon, pp. 1, 3, 6 (background), 17 (background); © Jemal Countess/WireImage/Getty Images, p. 2; © Todd Williamson/WireImage/Getty Images, p. 6; © Michael Williams/London Features International (USA) Ltd., p. 8; © George Ross/Getty Images, p. 10; Seth Poppel Yearbook Library, pp. 14, 15; © Rose Hartman/Globe Photos, Inc., p. 16; © Pierre Vauthey/CORBIS SYGMA, p. 17; © Kelly Jordan/Globe Photos, Inc., p. 18; © Marion Curtis/Time & Life Pictures/Getty Images, p.19; © Tammie Arroyo/Getty Images, p. 20; © Bill Davila/Retna Ltd., p. 22; © Ron Galella/WireImage/Getty Images, p. 23; © Lester Cohen/WireImage/Getty Images, p.25; © Frank Micelotta/Getty Images, p. 28; Kristin Callahan/Everett Collection, p. 29; © Michael Tran/FilmMagic/Getty Images, p. 31; © Bill Inoshita/CBS Photo Archive/Getty Images, p. 36; © Jonathan Fickles/Getty Images, p. 37; © Anthony Dixon/London Features International (USA) Ltd., p. 39. Front Cover: © Evan Agostini/Getty Images; © iStockphoto.com/yhloon (background).

Text copyright © 2009 by Lerner Publishing Group, Inc.

Lerner Publications Company
A division of Lerner Publishing Group, Inc.
241 First Avenue North
Minneapolis, MN 55401 U.S.A.

Website address: www.lernerbooks.com

Library of Congress Cataloging-in-Publication Data

Hill, Anne E., 1974–
      Tyra Banks : from supermodel to role model / by Anne E. Hill.
         p.   cm. — (Gateway biographies)
      Includes bibliographical references and index.
      ISBN 978-1-57505-949-5 (lib. bdg. : alk. paper)
      1. Banks, Tyra—Juvenile literature. 2. Models (Persons)—United States—Biography—Juvenile literature. I. Title.
      HD6073.M77B3645 2009
      746.9'2092—dc22 [B]   2008008730

Manufactured in the United States of America
1 2 3 4 5 6 – BP – 14 13 12 11 10 09

CONTENTS

Tyra Banks career includes work as a model, actress, reality television producer, and talk show host. Here she attends a fashion event in 2007.

t could have been a supermodel's worst nightmare—major newspapers and magazines running an unflattering photo with headlines calling her fat. Two-time *Sports Illustrated* cover girl Tyra Banks never imagined it would happen to her. She had been called curvy before. But she was shocked as she sat at her home computer one night and searched the Internet for her image.

Tyra saw the pictures of herself in a one-piece bathing suit on a beach in Australia. The headlines included "Thigh-ra Banks," "America's Next Top Waddle," and "Tyra Porkchop." Tyra wasn't embarrassed. She was angry. True, she had gained 30 pounds since her days on the catwalks of Paris. But the current talk show host and creator of the hit *America's Next Top Model* was a healthy five feet ten inches tall and weighed 161 pounds. She also believed that the magazines doctored the photos to make her look heavier than she actually was. "It was such a strange meanness and rejoicing that people had when thinking that was what my body looked like," thirty-three-year-old Tyra said.

8

Tyra worried about the effect the pictures would have on her self-esteem and her career. But she was even more worried about the effect they would have on the young fans that saw her as a role model. "I get so much mail from young girls who say 'I look up to you, you're not as skinny as everyone else, I think you're beautiful," she explained. "So when they say that my body is 'ugly' and 'disgusting,' what does that make those girls feel like?"

The self-esteem and weight concerns of her young fans prompted Tyra to start her TZONE (Tyra Zone) Foundation in 1999. The foundation helps disadvantaged girls deal with their insecurities about various issues. Two of the most common are concerns about looks and weight. Tyra hoped to prove a point about her photos to the girls in her foundation and her other fans. She appeared on her TV show wearing the

Tyra started the TZONE Foundation to help young girls feel better about themselves and their bodies.

bathing suit shown in the photos. Her audience cheered as Tyra struck different poses. She declared, "[I]f I had lower self-esteem, I would probably be starving myself right now. That's exactly what is happening to women all over this country." The controversy created one of Tyra's catch phrases and inspired a popular segment on her show called "So What!" "If I weigh 161 pounds or have cellulite on my butt, so what! I think I'm beautiful, and if you have a problem with that, so what!" she cried. Tyra has known firsthand about weight issues and name calling. She had come full circle since her teen years in California.

California Girl

Tyra Lynne Banks was born to Carolyn and Don Banks on December 4, 1973. The family also included Tyra's six-year-old brother Devin. The Banks family led a comfortable life in the Los Angeles suburb of Inglewood, California. Her father was a computer consultant. Her mother was a medical photographer. In her ocean-side neighborhood, Tyra enjoyed the company of extended family, friends, and neighbors. She claims she was a "daddy's girl" who got everything she wanted from her father.

Tyra's favorite childhood memory is of staying with her great-grandmother during the summer and watching soap operas all day.

Downtown Los Angeles, California, is shown here in 1980. Tyra grew up in Inglewood, a suburb of Los Angeles.

She has also said that her love for good food started early on. Family celebrations at the Banks house involved gathering around the dinner table and enjoying lots of homemade dishes—fried chicken, candied yams, ribs, pork chops, and honeyed ham. "I was taught to enjoy food, not to fear it," Tyra recalled. This love of food and family continues for Tyra. And she admits that she doesn't always eat the healthy stuff.

Tyra's mom, Carolyn, also loved good food, and she loved to exercise. She was an early role model for her young daughter. Tyra remembers watching her mom and her mother's friends working out together at their home. Soon Tyra was joining in too.

About the same time that she started to exercise, six-year-old Tyra discovered another secret to staying healthy—not smoking. One day, while playing at a friend's house, she came upon a lit cigarette in an ashtray. Curious, she lifted the cigarette to her lips and inhaled. Little Tyra swallowed a mouthful of smoke. She felt a painful burning in her lungs. Tyra vowed she would never try smoking again. It's a promise she has kept. And she has urged young people to follow her lead as well.

Young Tyra lost her maternal grandmother, fifty-year-old Florine London, to lung cancer. This was another reason why Tyra never smoked or promoted cigarettes.

In 1979 Tyra's happy childhood was rattled when her parents announced they were divorcing. Don Banks moved to a nearby apartment. Tyra stayed in the same private school she had started attending a year earlier. Her parents remained friendly. That made things easier for Tyra and Devin. The children also enjoyed the benefits of two birthday celebrations and two sets of Christmas presents.

Four years later, Carolyn announced she was remarrying. Ten-year-old Tyra wasn't sure she wanted a stepfather. She had difficulty adjusting at first. Her new stepdad was a high school graphic arts teacher named Clifford Johnson Jr. He was stricter than her dad had been. Clifford made sure Tyra and Devin had more household chores than before. Although she resented her stepdad's new rules at first, Tyra soon grew to love him. She was glad to see how happy he made her mother.

An Awkward Adolescence

Soon after her mother remarried, ten-year-old Tyra started bullying other girls at her small private school. She relates the bullying to her fights with her brother. Being older, he won almost every time. Tyra took her frustrations out on her classmates. "There were about ten girls in my fourth-grade class, and I was the leader of the pack," Tyra admitted. "The other girls would listen to whatever I said. I was popular, gossipy—and if I didn't want one of the other girls

> "Experiencing the pain of being picked on turned me around. It turned out that the best things [to happen to me] in my life were to be made fun of, and to have no friends, and to feel miserable every single day."
> —Tyra Banks in "Confessions of a Former Mean Girl"

to be in the clique anymore, for whatever tiny little reason, I voted her out." In front of the whole class, Tyra even told another student that she smelled.

But Tyra's time as the popular girl ended when she transferred to a large public middle school. It's hard to imagine the former supermodel being anything but beautiful. But Tyra shot up three inches and lost thirty pounds one summer. She became gawky and skinny. Her friends could hardly recognize her. "I went from being the popular girl who looked normal to being considered a freak." Kids called her Giraffe, Olive Oyl, and even Ethiopian. (In the 1980s, people in the United States became aware of the famine taking place in Ethiopia. They saw many photos of the starving people in that country.) Tyra became very shy. She didn't even want to get dressed for gym class. Getting braces and glasses didn't help Tyra feel better about her appearance. In other words, her early teenage years were not her happiest ones.

Finally, after a few years of feeling awkward and eating many fattening meals to gain weight, Tyra began to fill out. She started to get the curves that the other girls had. And she got some of her confidence back. Tyra also discovered that she had a flair for fashion. She enjoyed searching thrift shops to find clothes like the ones she saw in fashion magazines. One of Tyra's friends noticed her flair for fashion and her new figure. She urged Tyra to start modeling. With her flawless caramel skin and striking green eyes, many people thought Tyra was

14

beautiful. But Tyra herself wasn't completely sure. She still felt slightly insecure about her appearance. But she was interested in the world of fashion and world travel.

After a year of considering the idea, sixteen-year-old Tyra decided to go for it. Her photographer mom took some pictures of her for a modeling portfolio. Then Tyra started making the rounds at the local agencies.

Early Modeling Days

Tyra faced rejection at first. That was frustrating and humiliating. "I'd leave these places crying," Tyra remembered. "But my mom said, 'Look, if it's really something you want to do, use the rejection as motivation.'" Tyra did just that. She found an agency that thought she had a future in runway modeling (modeling the new designer clothes in front of an audience

This photo from Tyra's senior year shows her winning smile. Tyra was already working as a model while in school.

at seasonal fashion shows). But the agency thought she didn't have the face for print work (magazines and catalogs).

A year later, Tyra signed with the famous Elite Model Management, the largest modeling agency in the world. Tyra got some modeling jobs, including a print piece for *Seventeen* magazine in 1990. She juggled her jobs with her schoolwork. Although modeling was a new interest for Tyra, she was also determined to go to college. An excellent student, Tyra was accepted at local Loyola Marymount University for television and film studies.

Tyra put her college plans on hold, however, when she got the chance to go to Paris, France, and model haute couture (designer fashions). That was Tyra's big break and her chance to live in the capital of the fashion world. Working in Paris was also Tyra's first

By 1989, Tyra was working in glamorous runway shows.

time on her own. In the beginning, Tyra was lonely and homesick. But soon she started exploring the city and having fun. The experience was one she has never forgotten. "It made me aware of my true inner strengths and helped me to hone my survival skills....It taught me to learn about myself, to ask questions like: 'Who am I? What is my philosophy of life? What truly makes me happy?'"

In Paris, Tyra appeared in twenty-five runway shows for world-famous designers. They included Ralph Lauren, Coco Chanel, Oscar de la Renta, and Yves Saint Laurent. Tyra also appeared on her first magazine cover in Europe.

Tyra models an evening gown at a 1992 fashion show for designer Yves Saint Laurent in Paris.

She may have been a newcomer to the world of fashion, but the fashion world was taking notice of her unique look. "When I started modeling, I definitely wasn't the prettiest girl in the room. I was tall, skinny, and had a huge forehead—a little odd looking. But the fashion industry embraced me because I wasn't so typical," she recalled.

In October 1992, Tyra returned home as a well-known model. She had her own money and a hot career. But instead of partying and jet setting as many other young models did, Tyra decided to stay grounded. She wanted to be smart about her future. At the age of nineteen, she started her own company, Ty Girl Corporation. She hired her mom as her manager. Her dad Don was her financial adviser, and her cousin ran her fan club. Tyra also began to share some of her good fortune. She established the Tyra Banks Scholarship for African American girls at her old high school, Immaculate Heart.

Tyra and her mother, Carolyn, pose for a photo in 1993. Tyra hired her mother as her manager when she returned from Paris.

Tyra became a spokesmodel for makeup manufacturer Cover Girl. Here she poses next to a display of Cover Girl products.

Makeup and Movies

Tyra appeared on the covers of major U.S. magazines such as *Vogue, Elle, Esquire,* and *Cosmopolitan.* She traveled for jobs all over the world. The work was exciting and exhausting. But not until Tyra won a contract with top makeup manufacturer Cover Girl did she realize that she had truly arrived in the modeling world. She agreed to appear in both print and television ads for the company, just like former supermodels Cheryl Tiegs and Christie Brinkley. She was only the third African American model to sign with Cover Girl.

The same year she started working for Cover Girl, Tyra also decided to try acting. She admits that she never enjoyed getting her picture taken or posing. She told talk show host Larry King, "[I] liked the finished product [in modeling]. I did not like creating the product. But what I did like was the runway, because I felt like I was a big ham and I can just pounce on the runway." The idea of acting and getting to be an even bigger "ham" was very appealing to Tyra. In 1993 she played Will Smith's girlfriend on the sitcom *The Fresh Prince of Bel-Air*. The following year, she moved to the big screen. She had a role in the film *Higher Learning*, directed by John Singleton. Tyra played a student-athlete. She lost twelve to fifteen pounds training for the part. She enjoyed getting into character and becoming someone else on-screen. She also had a romantic relationship with Singleton. It lasted more than a year before they broke up.

Tyra planned to do more films if the right ones were offered. But she was clear about the roles she didn't want to play—girls who were just a pretty face. She wanted to be strong and show women—especially African American women—in a positive light.

Tyra and her *Higher Learning* director, John Singleton, dated for more than a year.

In addition to her roles in films, Tyra has also starred in music videos. They include Lionel Richie's "Don't Wanna Lose You," Michael Jackson's "Black or White," George Michael's "Too Funky," and Tina Turner's "Love Thing."

Breaking Barriers

In 1996 Tyra gave African American women a reason to be proud. She became the first black model to appear on the cover of the annual *Sports Illustrated* swimsuit issue. That same year, twenty-three-year-old Tyra also became the first woman to appear on the cover of *GQ* (*Gentlemen's Quarterly*). The honors were even more rewarding since Tyra had gained some weight. Her modeling agency had been pressuring her to lose weight. Once too thin, Tyra began losing jobs because she was bigger than other models. (She was five feet ten inches tall and weighed just 126 pounds at the time!) She remembered being embarrassed as two seamstresses at a show in Milan, Italy, talked about her weight. They called her *grasso*, which is "fat" in Italian. "If some designer had said it, it would hurt—but it hurt even more because maternal women were saying it," Tyra said.

Tyra was determined not to struggle with her weight anymore. She told her agency to find her jobs where her curves were viewed as an advantage rather than a drawback. Her plan worked. Soon, Tyra landed a major

Tyra models lingerie from Victoria's Secret. She signed a contract with the company in 1997.

contract with Victoria's Secret, a popular and well-known lingerie company. She earned about $4 million. Tyra became one of the popular chain stores' most famous faces (and bodies) in their mail-order catalogs. She was also their first African American cover model. Despite being heavier than other models, Tyra won the well-known Michael Award for Supermodel of the Year in 1997.

Author and Volunteer

Tyra liked to win awards for her modeling. But she wanted to make sure her young fans knew that beauty was more than skin deep. Almost since she could write, Tyra had kept journals filled with her memories, hopes, fears, disappointments, and things she had done and learned. Getting her thoughts down on paper was a great way to get rid of stress at the end of the day.

Looking back at the journals she had kept as a teen, Tyra realized that her experiences were very much like those of her teen fans. Tyra decided to write a book for her young fans. The book was dedicated to helping them feel better about themselves "inside and out." *Tyra's Beauty Inside & Out* hit bookstore shelves in early spring 1998. The magazine *School Library Journal* named it one of the Best Books of 1998.

More important, however, Tyra's young fans learned about Tyra's thoughts on life. In her book, Tyra discussed difficult topics such as drinking and smoking. She also addressed body image, self-esteem, sex, issues with parents, and school problems. She included letters people had sent to her as well as tips from her friends. Tyra wrote the book as if she were talking to a good friend. She wrote: "Some of you may look at me and think, 'That girl never had an insecure day in her life.'

Tyra shows off her book, *Tyra's Beauty Inside & Out*, at an autograph session in 1998.

Well, I think my experiences will prove that you can't always judge a book by its cover (not even this one)."

Tyra's ability to communicate with her young fans made her a natural choice to promote volunteerism—working for free to help the community. Cover Girl and *Seventeen* magazine asked Tyra to honor the winners of their 1998 Volunteerism Awards in Washington, D.C. And she happily accepted. Since her career had taken off seven years earlier, Tyra had spent much of her time and money helping others.

In addition to the Tyra Banks Scholarship, Tyra also got involved with the Center for Children and Families in New York City. The center helps disadvantaged children. She visited the center, hung out with the kids, and helped them learn to read. She even did art projects with them. Tyra turned some of their artwork into a line of greeting cards. The profit went to the center to help fund its programs. She also started the KidShare toy drive at the center. Corporations and individuals donate toys to the center. Then the kids give them to one another.

At the Volunteerism Awards lunch, Tyra presented six young women with scholarships for their outstanding efforts to help others. Tyra was thrilled to speak to the crowd about a topic she held so close to her heart. "When we volunteer our time and talents to help others, we're the ones who truly benefit," she said. Tyra's own efforts to help others hadn't gone unnoticed either. In 1997 she received the Starlight Starbright Children's Foundation of California Friendship Award.

Tyra started her TZONE Foundation in 1999. At first it was a summer camp for at-risk girls. The girls learned to develop independence and self-esteem. TZONE has since become a foundation that raises and grants money to groups that help women. On the foundation's website, Tyra explained why she started her organization. She said, "I started TZONE with my own money because I feel I have a responsibility to raise the awareness of the needs, ambitions and accomplishments of women and girls and to encourage others to join me in funding outstanding community-based organizations that help women live into their full potential." TZONE funds go to groups such as the Downtown Women's Center of Los Angeles, Lower Eastside Girls Club of New York, and the Young Chicago Authors.

Tyra sits with girls attending her TZONE Youth Camp in 2005.

Bankable Productions

At just twenty-five years old, Tyra was a millionaire many times over. She had charity projects she believed in and a career she found fulfilling—most of the time. But Tyra wanted to be more than a model. "I never thought of modeling as an end—I always had a plan," she admitted. Tyra wanted to be a businesswoman. She wanted to be in charge of every part of her career. She looked at older supermodel Cindy Crawford as a role model. Crawford was a shapely model like Tyra. But she also had had big deals with the Pepsi soft-drink company and Revlon, a beauty products company. Then she moved from modeling to hosting MTV's *House of Style*, a program about fashion and the lives of supermodels.

From the age of eighteen, Tyra had always wanted to have her own talk show. "I knew when I was a model that I wanted to have a talk show because I always had a voice, and I always had something to say," she later said. In 1999 Tyra took her first steps toward that goal. She became a youth correspondent on *The Oprah Winfrey Show*. She was a semiregular on the talk show. And she learned a lot from watching Oprah in action. Tyra was even offered her own talk show by another network after her appearances on Oprah. But Tyra knew that she didn't have quite enough life experience to be the kind of television

Tyra's mentors: "My mother is my greatest mentor. Oprah is definitely a mentor, because she is the best at what she does and she has such an amazing heart and spirit."

host she wanted to be. "I thought I was too young, and hadn't experienced enough. And I was probably judgmental back then. I hadn't experienced real heartbreak," she explained.

Tyra decided to form her own production company, Bankable Productions. She was still modeling, acting, and writing, but Tyra wanted to lay the foundation for a television career. More and more people were watching reality television shows in the early 2000s. Shows such as *Survivor*, *American Idol*, and *The Real World* were big hits. Tyra had her own idea for a reality show about the modeling world. She took her idea to reality producer Ken Mok. He knew it would be an instant hit with young women under thirty-five. In 2003 *America's Next Top Model* started on UPN (which changed to the CW when the two networks combined). Although the show did not get much promotion on the network, ratings were high from the start—thanks to Tyra. "That spoke volumes to me about this connection she had with women. It was a lot deeper than just being a model," said James Paratore. He is the president of Time Warner's syndication unit, Telepictures.

Tyra and Time Warner executive James Paratore speak to reporters about *America's Next Top Model.*

On the show, Tyra and a team of modeling industry insiders put a group of thirteen hopeful models (chosen by Tyra) to the test. The would-be models go on various jobs. Each week one girl is cut from the competition. In the end, the winner gets a modeling contract.

Tyra could be tough on the potential models during the show. But behind the scenes, she treated them more like little sisters. "Whenever a girl was sent home, I used to go to her hotel room and talk to her for an hour. . . . I felt like I created this show, I plucked this girl out of her obscure life and put her here, and it is my responsibility to make sure that she's successful."

Although all the girls on the show couldn't be winners, the show itself was a big success. It was always in the top ten TV programs for eighteen- to thirty-four-year-old females. During the seventh season in 2006, the last show of *America's Next Top Model* won the biggest ratings in its network's history.

The show, however, did get some criticism. Many people saw Tyra as continuing the trend of very young, thin models, even though she spoke against how skinny the standard had become. After several seasons of trying to have fuller-figure models on the show, Tyra got her way in February 2007. Two plus-size models competed on the show. She hopes this change will help the modeling world embrace women with fuller figures.

America's Next Top Model winner Whitney Thompson and Tyra pose at a television network event in 2008. Thompson was the first plus-size model to win the modeling contract on *America's Next Top Model*.

Tyra, the singer? In 2003 Tyra hired Mariah Carey's manager, Benny Medina, to produce a single, "Shake Ya Body." While Tyra admits that her voice sounded "decent" in the song, she also said that "you shouldn't ever do something because you're only decent at it."

Talk Show Host

A painful romantic relationship with National Basketball Association (NBA) star Chris Webber helped Tyra understand how it felt to be at her worst. She felt that pain helped her understand other women going through romantic troubles and heartbreak. Tyra and Webber started dating in 2002. They were even briefly engaged before they broke up in 2004. Their high-powered careers and rumors that the Sacramento Kings forward cheated on the supermodel tore them apart. Tyra was hurt. She admits that she did not have very much self-esteem at the time.

Tyra's past boyfriends include director John Singleton, basketball player Chris Webber, and musician Seal.

Not long after her breakup with Webber, Tyra felt that she was up to the challenge of her own television show. She went to her business manager and said it was time. In 2005 *The Tyra Banks Show* begins. Tyra was

Tyra talks to the audience at a taping of *The Tyra Banks Show*.

both the host and a producer. Her production company Bankable Productions co-owns the show. She was very involved in all aspects of the show. She described it as "a woman's guide to life. It's topical, connected to the news, but we do fashion and fun stuff. It's like different pages or sections in a women's magazine. They're unique, but they all fit together under one cover."

Again, Tyra connected with her target audience— young women in their teens, twenties, and thirties. Many people said her show was like *The Oprah Winfrey Show*. Tyra was both flattered and terrified by the thought of being matched with the top talk show queen of the United States. "I lost a lot of sleep about that early on. The next Oprah! I don't compare. . . . The biggest thing about Oprah is her authenticity. She is so true. There is no pretense to her, and the audience knows it."

One of the reasons Tyra's show was a hit with young women viewers was because Tyra understood them. As a young teen, Tyra never imagined that the pain she went through then would lead to the compassionate woman she has become. She can relate to guests on her talk show who are insecure or the victims of bullying.

She showed her audience that she is far from perfect. She talked about her cellulite—the dimply fat cells under the skin that can give it a rippled look.

She also showed her audience pictures of herself that hadn't been retouched. Computers make it possible to change a model's appearance with the click of a mouse. Most models' photos are changed. They make the models appear thinner in places, smooth their skin tone, or get rid of a blemish or under-eye circles. Tyra knew that women were comparing themselves to female images that weren't real. She was angry that the modeling industry wasn't being honest with its audience. She said: "I feel like it's my responsibility to do something about it because I was in fashion for so long projecting an image that's so hard to live up to. An image that is manipulated and tweaked."

In 2005, the same year her talk show had started, Tyra decided to retire from professional modeling. She hasn't regretted her decision to leave that world behind. She even listed the good things about retirement on her talk show's website. They included no longer obsessing about cellulite. She was able to focus less on her looks and more on her thoughts.

Exercise and eating right also became less a part of her job and more a part of being healthy for herself. Tyra admits that she loves comfort food, such as ribs. And she always enjoys a good dessert. She also confesses that she has let months go by without working out, which she knows isn't good for her health. Tyra tries to exercise for an hour every day. She also tries to eat more fruits, veggies, and lean proteins, such as chicken, fish, and certain cuts of meat. "I do treadmill intervals—I mix walking and running. Or I just run outside." She's happy with her weight. She says it fluctuates between 148 and 162 pounds. Because Tyra is satisfied with her body image, she wants to help other women feel better about theirs. Part of the problem, Tyra believes, is women labeling and putting down other women. Instead, she wants women to embrace their differences and accept them.

Going Undercover

As her show gained popularity, Tyra introduced themes. For example, Tyra loved showing how looks can be deceiving. But she also enjoyed deceiving a bit herself. She did this by going undercover. She posed as an over-weight woman, a homeless person, a man, a stripper, and a frumpy woman. She called these ventures "social experiments." She loved to see how differently she was treated in each situation.

Sometimes the results were disappointing. When she wore a suit to make her appear to weigh 350 pounds, Tyra was shocked by how cruel people could be. She called poking fun at obese people "the last accepted form of discrimination." She was amazed that people would not look her in the eye. They would even laugh in front of her. Tyra got to take off the suit—and the appearance of 200 extra pounds—at the end of her daylong experiment. But people's mean reactions stayed with her.

Another of Tyra's undercover jobs involved some audience members as well as herself. In a November 2007 episode, three women who were unhappy with their appearance traded places with three women the audience thought were pretty. The unhappy women got makeovers. The makeovers made a difference in how they felt and in the way others treated them. The other group received "makeunders" to appear less attractive. Tyra got fake bushy eyebrows, moles, a wig, and a big-ger nose and teeth. The results were stunning. "The girls who had glam makeovers were standing straighter. Their attitudes attracted attention," Tyra said. "The other girls felt self-conscious and were unsocial."

Tyra's audiences liked seeing how Tyra was a real

person. She was more than just a model in a magazine. She was more like a girlfriend. Tyra welcomed her audience's input. She found that people were most honest online. Tyra created a special forum for her fans to meet and exchange ideas. In 2007 a website (tyrashow.com) introduced a virtual studio based on her show. Fans could log on and download some free software. Then they could become an interactive part of the show and even suggest future topics. Or they could just hang out and talk. They could also enjoy content found only on the website and hear about upcoming events and stories.

Tyra enjoys other talk shows besides her own. She likes watching Jon Stewart and Bill O'Reilly in addition to Oprah Winfrey.

Big Awards and a Big Move

Tyra worked hard both in front of the camera and behind the scenes as a producer of the program. It seemed to be paying off. During her second season, she and the show were nominated for six Daytime Emmy Awards. They included Outstanding Talk Show Host and Outstanding Talk Show. She was also nominated for a National Association for the Advancement of Colored People (NAACP) Image Award and a Gay and Lesbian Alliance against Defamation (GLAAD) Award. She received the Teen Choice Award for Choice TV Personality.

Tyra works as a producer on both *America's Next Top Model* and *The Tyra Banks Show*. Here she works backstage at *Top Model*. Tyra's work as both host and a producer was rewarded when *The Tyra Banks Show* was nominated for Daytime Emmy Awards for its second season.

Tyra was also named to *Time* magazine's list of "100 Most Influential People" for 2006 and 2007. Tyra had never felt more proud than when she saw a copy of the magazine. Tyra saw herself listed with people such as former president Bill Clinton and Holocaust survivor Elie Wiesel. "Just a year ago I was a model . . . walking down the runway . . . for Victoria's Secret. And now *Time* magazine is saying I'm one of the most influential people in the world?"

In fall 2007, after two successful seasons in Los Angeles, *The Tyra Banks Show* (and its star) moved to

New York City. Having been a California girl all her life, Tyra was excited about the change. The city energized her. She worked on making her apartment a nice oasis at the end of her long days. She also tried to make her show even more entertaining and informative for its viewers. "I'm trying to get them more interested in issues," Tyra said of her audience. "Things that affect their future, you know? My talk show has totally changed me and opened me. . . . It made me more aware."

That first season in New York, Tyra welcomed Democratic presidential hopeful Barack Obama for an exclusive interview. She saw Obama's appearance as a chance to get her young audience interested in voting and politics. But she didn't ask the typical candidate questions. Instead, Tyra whipped out a crystal ball. She asked Senator Obama what he saw. His answer was the White House. They talked about Obama's two daughters and his wife, Michelle. They discussed

Tyra stands with a crowd on a street in New York City while filming her show in 2008. *The Tyra Banks Show* moved to New York City for filming in 2007.

what music was on his iPod and who would play him in a movie based on his life. Obama also sent out a special message to Tyra's brother, Captain Devin Banks, who was serving with the U.S. Army in Afghanistan.

Tyra says her favorite things are: 1) Taking off all my makeup at night. I call it the best feeling in the world. 2) Telling people good news. 3) Finding out that one of my shows touched or changed somebody's life. 4) Running into friends from elementary or high school that I haven't seen since graduation. 5) Barbecue ribs (baby backs!).

Empowering Young Women

In November 2007, Tyra's "Bodyville" segment aired on her show. This new social experiment was an eye-opening one. Women of different ethnic groups and sizes dressed in nude-colored bodysuits. They gave one another one-word labels describing their appearance— "unhealthy," "athletic," or "couch potato." The women then gave one another jobs based on their appearances. The experience was humiliating and hurtful as the women labeled and put one another down. But getting to the truth was incredibly healing as well. Tyra thought it showed people's prejudices and taught them what they needed to work on.

In addition to her "Bodyville" episode, Tyra has run "Teenville." Teens did a similar experiment and learned the

Tyra *(left)* poses for a photo with a fan in New York City.

lessons that come with labeling. Tyra has also exposed modeling scams where young women put themselves in possibly dangerous positions to become models. She set up a fake agency that sent out a call for potential models. These models paid to be seen by the agency (something a real agency would never do). They even agreed to take off their clothes in front of these strangers. Tyra showed just how dangerous—and even deadly—the modeling world could be. Tyra wants to help teach young women how to respect and take care of themselves.

Although she is only in her thirties, Tyra has accomplished much. And she has even more projects on the horizon for Bankable Productions. These include a sitcom, a dramatic series, and a made-for-television movie. Whatever she decides to do next, Tyra is sure to work hard and achieve success. "I'm inspired by challenge," she said. "When someone tells me I can't do something, it only makes me want to accomplish it more."

IMPORTANT DATES

1973	Tyra Lynne Banks is born on December 4 in Inglewood, California.
1979	Her parents divorce.
1983	Her mother remarries.
1985	Tyra grows three inches and loses thirty pounds.
1989	She signs with Elite Model Management.
1991	She graduates from high school and travels to Paris.
1992	She creates her own corporation and starts a Tyra Banks Scholarship at Immaculate Heart High School.
1993	She signs a five-year-contract with Cover Girl cosmetics.
1996	She becomes the first African American woman to appear on the cover of *Sports Illustrated* swimsuit edition and the first woman to appear on the cover of *GQ*.

1997	She signs a contract with Victoria's Secret.
1998	She publishes *Tyra's Beauty Inside & Out*.
1999	She begins work as special correspondent on *The Oprah Winfrey Show* and starts TZONE Foundation.
2003	*America's Next Top Model* starts.
2005	*The Tyra Banks Show* begins, and Tyra retires from modeling.
2007	She receives six Emmy nominations for *The Tyra Banks Show* and moves to New York City.
2008	Honored with the Media Award at the BET Awards. *The Tyra Banks Show* won an Emmy for Oustanding Talk Show — Informative.

GLOSSARY

discrimination: prejudicial outlook, action, or treatment

empower: to give power or authority; enable

haute couture: exclusive, trend-setting women's fashions created
by top designers

lingerie: women's underclothing

mentor: a trusted guide or counselor

pretense: a claim not supported by fact

SOURCE NOTES

7   Allison Adato and Amy Elisa Keith, "Tyra Talks, *People*, January 24, 2007, 82.

8   Ibid.

9   Claudia Croft, "The Triumph of Tyra," London *Sunday Times*, February 11, 2007.

9   Claire Connors, "Why I Love My Body . . . Just the Way It Is," *Shape*, January 2007, 63.

10   Pam Levin, *Tyra Banks* (Broomall, PA: Chelsea House Publishers, 2000), 24.

12–13   Tyra Banks, "Confessions of a Former Mean Girl," *Teen People*, August 2005, 52.

13   Ibid.

14   Celeste Fremon, "Not Just Another Pretty Face," *Good Housekeeping*, October 2005, 64.

16   Levin, 48.

18   "Tyra Banks: Fun Fearless Female Babe Bio," *Cosmopolitan*, April 2005, 66.

19–20   Tyra Banks, "Tyra Banks, Speaks Out," interview by Larry King, *Larry King Live,* CNN, January 29, 2007.

21   Adato and Keith, 86.

23–24   Levin, 86.

24   Ibid.

25   TZONE Foundation, TZONE, 2008, http://tzonefoundation.org/message.html (2008).

26   Clarissa Cruz, "Looker Who's Talking," *Entertainment Weekly*, August 26, 2005, 50.

26   Allison J. Waldman, "Personal Touch Makes Tyra Unique," *Television Week*, January 10, 2005, 24.

27   Allison J. Waldman, "Personal Touch Makes Tyra Unique," *Television Week*, January 10, 2005, 24.

27   Cruz, 50.

27   Kiri Blakely, "Tyra Banks on It," *Forbes*, July 3, 2006, 120.

28   Nancy Jo Sales, "A Model Mogul," *Vanity Fair*, February 2007, 168.

30   Blakely, 120.

31   Andy Serwer, "From Top Model to Young Oprah," *Fortune*, February 20, 2006, 28.

31–32   Ibid., 28.

32   Sales, 168.

33   Connors, 63.

34   Sales, 168.

34   James Patrick Herman, "Tyra Banks," *InStyle*, October 2006, 478.

34   Eric Andersson, "Tyra's Big Makeunder," *US Weekly*, November 26, 2007, 76.

36   Sales, 168.

37   Ibid.

39   Gabrielle Gayagoy, "A Look Back with . . . Tyra Banks," *Shape*, June 2007, 34.

SELECTED BIBLIOGRAPHY

Adato, Allison, and Amy Elisa Keith. "Tyra Talks." *People*, January 24, 2007.

Andersson, Eric. "Tyra's Big Makeunder." *US Weekly*, November 26, 2007.

Banks, Tyra. "Confessions of a Former Mean Girl." *Teen People*, August 2005.

Blakely, Kiri. "Tyra Banks on It." *Forbes*, July 3, 2006.

Connors, Claire. "Why I Love My Body . . . Just the Way It Is." *Shape*, January 2007.

Cruz, Clarissa. "Looker Who's Talking." *Entertainment Weekly*, August 26, 2005.

Garcelon, Annie. "Tyra Banks." *Daily Variety*, July 30, 2007.

Herman, James Patrick. "Tyra Banks." *InStyle*, October 2006.

Keegan, Rebecca Winters. "Not Fat, But Happy." *Time*, February 26, 2007.

Purcell, Chris. "Tyra Banks' Moving to New York." *Television Week*, June 6, 2007.

Sales, Nancy Jo. "A Model Mogul." *Vanity Fair*, February 2007.

Serwer, Andy. "From Top Model to Young Oprah." *Fortune*, February 20, 2006.

Triggs, Charlotte, and Amy Elisa Keith. "My Favorite Summer Memory." *People*, May 24, 2006.

Wolf, Naomi. "Tyra Banks." *Time South Pacific*, May 4, 2007, Australia-New Zealand edition.

FURTHERREADING

Banks, Tyra, and Vanessa Thomas Bush. *Tyra's Beauty Inside &
Out*. New York: Harper-Collins Publishers, 1998.

Levin, Pam. *Tyra Banks*. Broomall, PA: Chelsea House Publishers,
2000.

tyrabanks.com
http://www.tyrabanks.com
Tyra's official website features her biography, photos, and
contact information. It also has sections on her television
show, production company, and her fans.

The Tyra Banks Show
http://www.tyrashow.com
The official site for *The Tyra Banks Show* offers show recaps,
a look at upcoming guests and topics, and ticket information.
It also has a large section for fans, featuring topics on news
events, beauty, dating, and other topics.

Tyra Banks–TZONE Foundation
http://www.tzonefoundation.org
The official website for Tyra's TZONE Foundation discusses
why it was created. It also tells which groups receive grants
and how groups can apply for assistance. The site also has a
message from Tyra and a news section.

INDEX

Page numbers in *italics* refer to illustrations.